Little Squiggle's Lake Adventure

By Laura Smetana and Stirling Hebda

Illustrated by Laura Smetana

Flying Cardinal Press, LLC

Text copyright © 2021 by Laura Smetana and Stirling Hebda
Illustrations copyright © 2021 by Laura Smetana
All rights reserved. Published by Flying Cardinal Press, LLC, Woodridge, IL.
No part of this book may be reproduced, stored in a retrieval system, or transmitted in any form or by any means, electronic, mechanical, photocopying, recording, or otherwise, without written permission of the publisher. For requests, please contact: info@flyingcardinalpress.com.
Library of Congress Control Number: 2021909868
ISBN: 978-1-7371409-1-7 (hardcover)
ISBN: 978-1-7371409-3-1 (paperback)
ISBN: 978-1-7371409-0-0 (e-book)
First Edition, August 2021
Cover and book design by Kath Grimshaw
Edited by Veronica Benduski and Meredith Tennant
Text set in True Sketch
The artwork in this book was created with watercolor and digital ink.

To my parents, who inspired a spirit of adventure, and Greg, for getting a kayak without asking (thank you)
—L.S.

To Shirley, for inspiring us to start watercoloring
—S.H.

"What should we do today?" Little Lou asked her best friend, Little Squiggle.

"Let's go to the lake!" said Little Squiggle. "We can try out my new kayak."

Little Lou had never been kayaking before. "Will there be sharks in the water?" she asked as they walked to the lake.

"Oh no!" laughed Little Squiggle. "Don't worry. There are just small fish in the water."

They climbed into the kayak and paddled away from the shore.

Soon, shimmering water surrounded them on all sides.

They paused to enjoy the view as they bobbed up and down on the choppy waves.

As the water calmed, Little Squiggle shouted, "Look! There's an island! Let's get closer to see the flowers."

"I'd love to," replied Little Lou.

Together, Little Squiggle and Little Lou paddled closer to the little island.

"Do you hear that beautiful music?" asked Little Lou with a smile.

Little Squiggle paused for a moment and closed his eyes. "I think it's coming from that other island with trees," he said. "Let's go see what it is!"

The music grew louder and louder as they paddled closer and closer to the rocky shore. They came to a stop as the kayak scraped across the gravel below.

"I have an idea!" said Little Squiggle. "We could use this rope." Little Squiggle tied one end of the rope to the kayak and placed three heavy rocks securely on the other end.

Afraid of falling in the water, Little Lou took a deep breath and slowly stepped onto shore with Little Squiggle's help. They began to explore the island to find out where the music had come from.

They found rocks covered in green algae,

beautiful flowers blowing in the breeze,

graceful feathers from island birds,

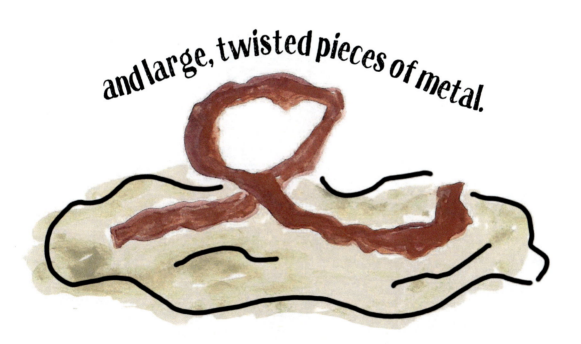

and large, twisted pieces of metal.

But no signs of music.

"Let's get a closer look," replied Little Squiggle. Step by step, they climbed up the hill to admire the unusual flower.

Suddenly, a little red bird landed on the flower and started singing the beautiful song they had heard from the shore.

When the little red bird finished singing, Little Squiggle and Little Lou clapped in admiration.
"Welcome to our island!" chirped the little red bird. "Follow me and I'll show you around."

The little red bird gave Little Squiggle and Little Lou a tour of the island. They went up, down, and all around until they had seen every tree, rock, and flower. Then it began to drizzle.

Little Squiggle and Little Lou's new friend led them back to the shore, but when they got there, the kayak was gone!

With a whoosh of air, the little red bird returned with a flock of feathered friends speeding behind him.

The birds flew over the water, dodging raindrops that poured from the sky. Together, they grasped the rope tightly with their feet and pulled the kayak back across the water.

"We did it! Thank you! Thank you!" cheered Little Squiggle and Little Lou. They hurried into the kayak and waved goodbye to their new friends. Together, they paddled back as fast as they could, while the rain drenched them from head to toe.

About the Author-Illustrator

Laura Smetana loves writing, painting, and kayaking with her family. As a kid, Laura was a self-described bookworm, and one of her favorite places is still the library. In the fifth grade, Laura created a book about a giraffe named Little Squiggle. After reading it to Stirling for bedtime, he said, "We should bring Little Squiggle back, Mom!" And that's what they did. This is their first book together. You can visit her at **www.laurasmetana.com.**

About the Author

Stirling Hebda is Laura's son and is still a kid. He enjoys playing video games, freeze tag, and sports, like soccer and rugby. When he isn't at school, Stirling loves eating snacks and competing in enthusiastic rock-paper-scissors battles to get the best seat in the kayak. He lives with his parents and robot dog and cat.

Made in the USA
Las Vegas, NV
28 November 2021